Contents

Introduction
to Course & Subjects

Course Outline

This is a four part course designed to help participants learn more about their faith and how to apply it to everyday life, how to study the Bible, explore theology and become more effective leaders.

The subjects and some of the elements covered are:

Bible: Jesus, The Bible & You –
* How to read the Bible devotionally and for study purposes
* Historical background to the Bible
* How to use all the Bible study tools
* How to get revelations from the Bible

Leadership: The Church & Your Leadership Journey – Learn effective leadership qualities and skills that can build your own life and the lives of others, seeing the kingdom of God move forward.

Lifestyle: Following Jesus –
* How to build a strong devotional life
* How to find your purpose in God
* How to live a life that can fulfil your purpose
* How to hear from God

Theology: Faith Foundations – Develop a personal theology in a biblical and thoughtful way that will be a blessing to you and your church community.

Learning Sessions

Once per week for 2½ hours which includes 2 teaching sessions, 1 application session and a 20min break (after session 1).

Teaching Sessions – each week will include 2 x 50 minute sessions in a lecture style.

Application Sessions – each week will consist of 1 x 25 minute group session where homework and previous teaching sessions will be used to stimulate discussion. These sessions will vary in activities including multimedia and role playing etc.

Homework

Each week you will get a small amount of work to complete at home. It should take about 20 minutes to complete and it will be used to stimulate discussion the following week during the group session. There are also some advanced questions for those who wish to do more in-depth study.

Bible Version

Throughout this course the New International Version (NIV) has been used unless otherwise specified.

Many translations can be viewed freely from websites such as: **www.biblegateway.com**, **www.biblestudytools.com** and **www.bible.cc** or on your mobile device using applications such as **YouVersion**. We encourage you to research and find what works best for you.

Before you commence spend a few moments to pray and ask the Holy Spirit to give you eyes to see what the Word is saying to you.

Bible
Jesus, The Bible & You

This subject gives a seven week overview of the life and significance of Jesus as described in the four gospels. It will also help you develop your Bible study skills.

Recommend Readings

If you want to get a deeper understanding of this subject, below are some recommended resources:

* A Short Life – **John Dickson** (Lion 2008)

* Bible Study Methods – **Rick Warren** (Zondervan 2006)

* How to Read the Bible for All It's Worth – **Gordon Fee and Douglas Stuart** (Zondervan 2003)

* How to Read the Bible Book by Book – **Gordon Fee and Douglas Stuart** (Zondervan 2002)

* The Life: A Portrait of Jesus – **J. John and Chris Walley** (Authentic 2006)

* Vintage Jesus – **Mark Driscoll and Gerry Breshears** (Crossways Books 2007)

* Today's New International Version Study Bible (Zondervan 2006)

Week¹

Introduction

Session 1 – Introduction to the Bible
The Bible as History
The Old and New Testaments
Your Bible

Break

Session 2 – The Life of Jesus and the Gospels
The Nature and Function of the Gospels
The Life and Geography of Jesus

Session 3 – Understanding and Applying the Bible

Homework – The Historical Setting
Reading Plan – Luke 1– 4

Session 1
Introduction to the Bible

The Bible As History

The Old and New Testaments

Old Testament

Pentateuch/Law

Genesis	Exodus	Leviticus	Numbers	Deuteronomy				

Historical Books

Joshua	Judges	Ruth	1 & 2 Samuel	1 & 2 Kings	1 & 2 Chronicles	Ezra	Nehemiah	Esther			

Poetic Books

Job	Psalms	Proverbs	Ecclesiastes	Song of Songs	

Prophetic Books

Isaiah	Jeremiah	Lamentations	Ezekiel	Daniel	Hosea	Joel	Amos	Obadiah	Jonah	Micah	Nahum	Habakkuk	Zephaniah	Haggai	Zechariah	Malachi

New Testament

Gospels				Acts	Paul's Letters										Other Letters					Apocalyptic
Matthew	Mark	Luke	John	Acts	Romans	1 & 2 Corinthians	Galatians	Ephesians	Philippians	Colossians	1 & 2 Thessalonians	1 & 2 Timothy	Titus	Philemon	Hebrews	James	1 & 2 Peter	1, 2 & 3 John	Jude	Revelation

Your Bible

It is best to work with a translation that uses "dynamic equivalence" but have examples of the other types for comparison and reference.

Literal/Formal Translations	Dynamic Equivalents Mediating	Functional Paraphrases

The diagram below shows the two different ways in which translation takes place: i) Translating word for word
ii) Translating whole thoughts for meaning

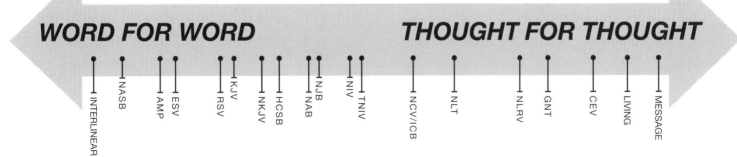

Session 2
The Life of Jesus and the Gospels

Outcomes

By the end of this session, you will be able to:
* Understand the nature of the gospels and their function
* Establish a possible timeline for Jesus' life
* Recognise the geography of Jesus' ministry

The Nature and Function of the Gospels

The Life and Geography of Jesus

Session 3
Understanding and Applying the Bible

In groups read Matthew 15:21-28.

Background research

What information do you need in order to work out the significance of this encounter in the 1st century?
e.g., What was significant about the woman and where she lived?

What did the interaction between Jesus and the woman reveal about Jesus' mission focus at this point?

Note: If you have access to the Internet or a Study Bible research the answers. Otherwise simply list the questions that arise from reading this passage.

Application

What have you learned from this passage that you can apply practically to your own life? (e.g., in relation to faith, Jesus' response to the woman etc.)

Homework

The Historical Setting

How did the Jews think of themselves at the time of Jesus? What would they have thought about the fact that they were ruled by the Roman Empire, not their own king?

What was Luke's intention for writing the Gospel of Luke? (Luke 1:1-4) What relevance might that have for us today?

Advanced Work

Do a search on the internet to answer this question: How did the Romans come to rule Israel/Judea at the time of Jesus?

_____

_____

_____

_____

_____

_____

_____

_____

_____

_____

Reading Plan

To take you through the Gospel of Luke over the seven weeks of the course. This will give you a great understanding of the life of Jesus.

This Week's Reading Plan – Luke 1-4

Week²

Session 1
Background to the Life of Jesus (Part 1)

Historical Overview of the Inter-Testamental Period

Three Major Concerns in 1st Century Judaism

Session 2

Background to the Life of Jesus (Part 2)

Outcomes

By the end of this session, a student:

* Can recognise God's timing and fulfillment of prophecies
* Can have an understanding of the different types of people living in 1st century Israel
* Can apply some of the 1st century responses to a 21st century setting

The Timing of the Plan of God

PROPHECY (Old Testament)	FULFILLED (New Testament)
Jesus would be of the house of David **2 Samuel 7:12-16; Jeremiah 23:5; Psalm 89:3-4**	**Genealogy** Matthew 1, Luke 1:27,32,69
He will be born in a small city called Bethlehem, specifically the one formerly known as Ephratah **Micah 5:2**	Matthew 2:3-6; Luke 2:4-6
He will be born of a virgin **Isaiah 7:14**	Matthew 1:22,23; Luke 1:14,15
He will be a priest after the order of Melchisedek **Psalm 110:4**	Hebrews 5:6
He will enter Jerusalem riding a donkey (the colt of an ass) **Zechariah 9:9**	Matthew 21:5; Luke 19:32-37
A messenger (a man of the wilderness) will prepare the way for Him **Isaiah 40:3; Malachi 3:1**	**John the Baptist** Matthew 3:1-3; 11:10; Luke 1:17
The price of His betrayal will be thirty pieces of silver **Zechariah 11:12**	Matthew 27:3-10
Crucifixion foretold **Psalm 22:14-17**	Matthew 27:26,39,44; John 20:25
They will divide His clothing and cast lots for them **Psalm 22:18**	John 19:23-24
He will be given vinegar and gall to drink **Psalm 69:21**	Matthew 27:34,48
He will be raised from the dead **Psalm 16:10**	Acts 2:31
He will ascend into heaven **Psalm 68:18**	Acts 1:9
He will be seated at the right hand of God **Psalm 110:1**	Hebrews 1:3
He will be the Son of God **Psalm 2:7**	Matthew 3:17

Different Groups of People in Israel in the 1st Century

Session 3

Applying the 1st Century Responses to a 21st Century Setting

Read the following section on the Sadducees –

The Sadducees supported the Hasmoneans and were almost entirely from the aristocracy. Many were from priestly families (probably the name Sadducee comes from the priestly family of 'Zadokites' (cf. 2 Samuel 8:17). They built up great wealth and became corrupt in their use of it in the way that they administered the temple. They did not protest about the Roman occupation of Israel. Because they were so tied to the temple they did not survive the fall of Jerusalem in 70BC.

Beliefs: Sadducees rejected the oral law and believed that only the five books of Moses (Torah) were binding. They denied immortality, resurrection, angels and demons. They strongly emphasised the freedom of the human will. Jesus repeatedly criticised the Sadducees.

Encounters with Jesus: Mark 11:15-18: Cleansing of Temple Sadducees introduced money changers into the temple precincts instead of housing them in nearby Kidron Valley.

Now read Mark 12:18-28 and answer the following questions –

What did the Sadducees believe about the resurrection and the supernatural?

_____

_____

What was significant about the way Jesus answered them?

Why would the teachers of the law be pleased at Jesus' answer? (v.28)

Discuss what we can learn from the way Jesus handled the Sadducees.

Application

How do you handle discussions with non-Christians who seem to be expert on the Bible? What about Jehovah's Witnesses etc.? Note that Jesus started from where the Sadducees were. He answered them out of the books that they believed.

What are the areas that you feel weakest with regards to answering the previous questions? Discuss some possible answers that you could give.

Discuss how you could answer a Jewish friend on the question of whether Jesus was the Messiah using the Old Testament as your evidence. Note: Make use of Messianic passages and prophecies that Jesus fulfilled.

Homework

The Start of Jesus' Life and Ministry

Read John 1:1-18. What do you learn about Jesus and His coming?

Look at the words of some popular carols and choose some lines that you feel really capture and express the incarnation and birth of Jesus. (Suggested carols to research on the Internet include: O Come All Ye Faithful; Hark The Herald Angels Sing; Once In Royal David's City; O Little Town Of Bethlehem)

Advanced Work

Find the passages in each of the gospels where Jesus is baptised and then goes into the wilderness to be tempted by Satan. What similarities and differences do you notice between each passage?

_____

_____

_____

_____

_____

_____

_____

_____

_____

_____

_____

This Week's Reading Plan – Life of Jesus (Luke 5-8)

Week³

Introduction

Session 1 – The Early Years (Part 1)
The Birth of Jesus
The Baptism of Jesus

Break

Session 2 – The Early Years (Part 2)
The Temptation in the Desert
The Calling of the Disciples

Session 3 – Biographical Study on John the Baptist

Homework – The Kingdom of God
Reading Plan – Luke 9-12

Session 1
The Early Years (Part 1)

Outcomes

By the end of this session, you will be able to:
* Have an understanding of the historical, human and theological background to the birth of Jesus
* Recognise the place of John the Baptist in Jesus' life and ministry
* Understand the significance of Jesus' baptism

The Birth of Jesus

The Baptism of Jesus

Session 2
The Early Years (Part 2)

Outcomes

By the end of this session, you will be able to:
* Describe how Jesus' temptations were both unique to Jesus and common to human experience
* Apply the lessons learned from Jesus' temptations to their own life
* Outline the make-up and calling of the disciples
* Apply lessons learned from their responses to that call to their own life

The Temptation in the Desert

The Calling of the Disciples

Session 3
Biographical Study on John the Baptist

Read the set of passages on John the Baptist that your group has been assigned.
Discuss and summarise the main lesson(s) that you feel was taught or illustrated by John the Baptist's life in these passages.

Passages on John the Baptist

Birth of John the Baptist: Luke 1:5-15,39-45
Ministry of John the Baptist: Matthew 3:1-15;Mark 1:2-9; Luke 3:1-21; John 1:29-35
John's testimony about Jesus: John 1:6,7,15-28; John 3:22-30; John 5:33-36
Arrest and execution of John the Baptist: Mark 1:14; Luke 3:19,20; Matthew 11:2-6; Luke 7:18-23; Matthew 14:1-12; Mark 6:14-29; Luke 9:7-9
John the Baptist compared to Elijah: Matthew 11:7-19; Mark 9:11-13; Luke 7:24-35

Write out a personal application based on what you have learned. Reflect on the following questions:

★ Did I see anything of myself in John the Baptist's life?

★ Did I see any of my weaknesses? If so, what?

★ Did I see any of my strengths? If so, what?

★ What impressed me most about John the Baptist from these passages?

★ What do I intend to do about what I have learned?

Homework

The Kingdom of God

Write a definition of what you understand by the kingdom of God that would be understood by a new Christian.

During the weekend service you attend listen for references to the kingdom of God. What were some of those references?

Advanced Work

Do a thematic study on the kingdom of God in Mark's Gospel. Do this by following these steps:
Use a concordance, Bible software or internet Bible to list all of the verses in Mark's Gospel that mention the kingdom.

Read through these verses a few times, noting down the various ideas or themes you notice.

_____

_____

_____

_____

_____

_____

_____

_____

_____

_____

_____

_____

_____

This Week's Reading Plan – Life of Jesus (Luke 9-12)

Week⁴

Introduction

Session 1 – The Kingdom of God (Part 1)
Jesus as Messiah
The Kingdom of God (Part 1)

Break

Session 2 – The Kingdom of God (Part 2)
The Parables of the Kingdom
The People of the Kingdom
The Significance of the Kingdom for 21st Century Believers

Session 3 – Reading and Applying the Parables Correctly

Homework – The Beatitudes (Matthew 5:1-12)
Reading Plan – Luke 13-16

Session 1
The Kingdom of God (Part 1)

Outcomes

By the end of this session, you will be able to:
* Understand the background to the title Messiah and how Jesus reinterpreted it
* Describe the significance of the kingdom of God in Jesus' ministry
* Recognise the present and future elements of the kingdom

Jesus as Messiah

The Kingdom of God (Part 1)

Session 2
The Kingdom of God (Part 2)

Outcomes

By the end of this session, you will be able to:
* Understand how parables work and need to be interpreted
* Apply parables to their own lives
* Explain who the people of the kingdom are and why
* Apply the teaching on the kingdom to their own lives

The Parables of the Kingdom

The People of the Kingdom

The Significance of the Kingdom for 21st Century Believers

Session 3
Reading and Applying Parables Correctly

In groups read **Matthew 13:33 – Parable of Yeast**.
What is the message of this parable? Note Jesus' introduction to the parable for a clue to the subject matter.
Is there anything you need to know in terms of background information?
How could you re-tell this parable using a 21st century image?

_____

_____

_____

_____

Now read the two parables in **Matthew 13:31,32 and Matthew 13:44.** What are the main points of each parable? How can we apply them to our lives today?

_____

_____

_____

_____

_____

_____

_____

_____

Homework

The Beatitudes (Matthew 5:1-12)

Fill in the chart on the following pages selecting four phrases from the Beatitudes that are words you would like to compare across other translations. Selected translations are provided, but feel free to use your own choice.

As you notice how different versions translate the Beatitudes, how does this comparison deepen your understanding of the passage?

Take a few moments to consider the message of the Beatitudes and pray as you feel led by the Holy Spirit.

Matthew 5:3-10

New International Version	The Message	New Living Translation
He said: 3 Blessed are the poor in spirit, for theirs is the kingdom of heaven. 4 Blessed are those who mourn, for they will be comforted. 5 Blessed are the meek, for they will inherit the earth. 6 Blessed are those who hunger and thirst for righteousness, for they will be filled. 7 Blessed are the merciful, for they will be shown mercy. 8 Blessed are the pure in heart, for they will see God. 9 Blessed are the peacemakers, for they will be called children of God. 10 Blessed are those who are persecuted because of righteousness, for theirs is the kingdom of heaven.	3 You're blessed when you're at the end of your rope. With less of you there is more of God and his rule. 4 You're blessed when you feel you've lost what is most dear to you. Only then can you be embraced by the One most dear to you. 5 You're blessed when you're content with just who you are—no more, no less. That's the moment you find yourselves proud owners of everything that can't be bought. 6 You're blessed when you've worked up a good appetite for God. He's food and drink in the best meal you'll ever eat. 7 You're blessed when you care. At the moment of being 'care-full,' you find yourselves cared for. 8 You're blessed when you get your inside world—your mind and heart—put right. Then you can see God in the outside world. 9 You're blessed when you can show people how to cooperate instead of compete or fight. That's when you discover who you really are, and your place in God's family. 10 You're blessed when your commitment to God provokes persecution. The persecution drives you even deeper into God's kingdom.	3 God blesses those who are poor and realize their need for him,[a] for the Kingdom of Heaven is theirs. 4 God blesses those who mourn, for they will be comforted. 5 God blesses those who are humble, for they will inherit the whole earth. 6 God blesses those who hunger and thirst for justice,[b] for they will be satisfied. 7 God blesses those who are merciful, for they will be shown mercy. 8 God blesses those whose hearts are pure, for they will see God. 9 God blesses those who work for peace, for they will be called the children of God. 10 God blesses those who are persecuted for doing right, for the Kingdom of Heaven is theirs.

Verse, Word or Phrase	New International Version	The Message	New Living Translation

Verse, Word or Phrase	New International Version	The Message	New Living Translation

Advanced Work

Read the entire Sermon on the Mount (Matthew 5-7).
Write one sentence on how each paragraph impacted you.

_____

_____

_____

_____

_____

_____

_____

_____

_____

_____

_____

_____

This Week's Reading Plan – Life of Jesus (Luke 13-16)

Week⁵

Introduction

Session 1 – Jesus' Teaching (Part 1)
Jesus' Attitude to the Law
Jesus' Teaching on Grace

Break

Session 2 – Jesus' Teaching (Part 2)
The Setting of the Sermon on the Mount
The Sermon on the Mount and the Christian Life

Session 3 – Applying a New Testament Narrative to Our Own Lives

Homework – Jesus' Miracles
Reading Plan – Luke 17-20

Session 1
Jesus' Teaching (Part 1)

Outcomes

By the end of this session, you will be able to:
* Describe Jesus' attitude to the Law
* Understand the relationship of law and grace in Jesus' teaching
* Apply Jesus' teaching on law and grace to their own lives

Jesus' Attitude to the Law

Jesus' Teaching on Grace

Session 2

Jesus' Teaching (Part 2)

Outcomes

By the end of this session, you will be able to:
* Describe the context of the Sermon on the Mount
* Understand the implications of the sermon for the Christian life
* Apply the Sermon on the Mount to their own lives

The Setting of the Sermon on the Mount

The Sermon on the Mount and the Christian Life

Session 3

Applying a New Testament Narrative
to Our Own Lives

Read Luke 7:36-50 in groups. Follow the journeys of Simon the Pharisee and the sinful woman in the narrative. Bear in mind the following points on narratives:

* What people do in narratives is not necessarily a good example for us but is often the opposite
* All narratives are selective and incomplete but contain everything that the author, under the inspiration of the Holy Spirit, thought was important for us to know

Discuss the following questions:

What is the message of the parable that Jesus told Simon (Luke 7:40-43)? Which person in the narrative illustrates which debtor?

_____

_____

_____

_____

_____

Who do you identify with and why? (You may identify with more than one character or you may recognise how you have identified with one in the past and now identify with another)

_____

_____

_____

_____

_____

_____

_____

What are the major positive or negative qualities that you see in each of these people?

_____

_____

_____

_____

_____

_____

_____

What can you take away from the example of any of these people and apply to your own life? Is there something you need to change? Is there something you need to do?

_____

_____

_____

_____

_____

_____

When reading a narrative we can often forget that the one person we are told to imitate is Jesus. What do we learn from this narrative about Jesus' responses that we can imitate?

_____

_____

_____

_____

_____

_____

Homework

Read quickly through John 1:19-12:50 (often called the Book of Signs). Read and list every miracle that is described in these chapters.

Write down any thoughts that you have about the significance of these miracles. Pay special attention to what either Jesus or the author, John, have to say.

_____

_____

_____

_____

_____

_____

Write down your own personal experience of the miraculous. Ask your family and friends about their experiences.

_____

_____

_____

_____

This Week's Reading Plan – Life of Jesus (Luke 17-20)

Advanced Work

List all the miracles that are described in all four gospels. Make a note of those that are described in more than one gospel.

Week⁶

Introduction

Session 1 – Jesus' Miracles
The Source of Jesus' Miracles
The Types of Miracles
The Significance of Jesus' Miracles

Break

Session 2 – The Final week
The Events of the Final Week
Reflections from the Last Supper
Lessons from Gethsemane
The Arrest and Trial of Jesus

Session 3 – The Four Accounts of the Entry into Jerusalem

Homework – The Cross
Reading Plan – Luke 21-24

Session 1
Jesus' Miracles

Outcomes

By the end of this session, you will be able to:
* Understand the divine authority and source of Jesus' miracles and teaching
* Outline the different types of miracles
* Describe the significance of Jesus' miracles and apply that to their own lives

The Source of Jesus' Miracles

The Types of Miracles

The Significance of Jesus' Miracles

Session 2
The Final Week

Outcomes

By the end of this session, you will be able to:
* Describe a possible outline for Jesus' final week
* Understand the significance of the Last Supper for Jesus and for 21st century Christians
* Describe the events in the garden of Gethsemane and apply the lessons learned to their own lives
* Outline the events of the betrayal and trial of Jesus

The Events of the Final Week

Reflections from the Last Supper

Lessons from Gethsemane

The Arrest and Trial of Jesus

Session 3
The Four Accounts of the Entry Into Jerusalem

Read Matthew 21:19; Mark 11:1-10; Luke 19:28-40; John 12:12-19.
Make notes on each passage and what is the same and what is different or added. Then:

✱ Discuss the significance of Jesus' entry into Jerusalem.
✱ Discuss the significance of what is added in different accounts for your understanding of this event.
✱ Discuss the response of the crowd in contrast to their response when Jesus was before Pilate only a few days later (Matthew 27:15-23). What do you notice?
✱ If you were leading a Bible study on this event what would you draw from it to apply to a 21st century situation?

_____

_____

_____

_____

_____

Homework

The Cross

Read Isaiah chapter 53 in the Message Version. Write down the ways in which Jesus fulfilled this prophecy.

Write a prayer or a journal entry that reflects on this passage.

Advanced Work

Using a Bible with cross-references look up all the occasions when Isaiah chapter 53 is quoted in the New Testament.

This Week's Reading Plan – Life of Jesus (Luke 21-24)

Week⁷

Introduction

Session 1 – The Crucifixion
The Offence of the Cross
Jesus' View of the Cross
Jesus' Words on the Cross

Break

Session 2 – The Resurrection
Background
Arguments For and Against the Resurrection
The Significance of The Resurrection

Session 3 – Jesus' Post-Resurrection Commands

Session 1
The Crucifixion

By the end of this session, you will be able to:
* Explain why the cross offended both Jews and Gentiles and still offends today
* Describe Jesus' understanding of the necessity of the cross
* Apply Jesus' words on the cross to their own lives.

The Offence of the Cross

Jesus' View of the Cross

Jesus' Words on the Cross

Session 2
The Resurrection

Outcomes

By the end of this session, you will be able to:

* Outline the historical and theological background to the resurrection
* Make some arguments for the historicity of the resurrection
* Understand the significance of the resurrection and apply it to their own situation

Background

Arguments For and Against the Resurrection

The Significance of The Resurrection

Session 3
Jesus' Post-Resurrection Commands

The Great Commission

Read Matthew 28:16-20

✱ Summarise the passage and think about its context in the book of Matthew.

✱ What do you need to apply to your life from this passage? **(Note that this is a command of Jesus, so it is NOT optional!)**

✱ Discuss how you can be practically part of fulfilling the Great Commission.